BILL BRIGHT

Heaven OR HELL

YOUR ULTIMATE CHOICE

NewLife
PUBLICATIONS

Heaven or Hell: Your Ultimate Choice

Published by
New*Life* Publications
A ministry of Campus Crusade for Christ
P.O. Box 620877
Orlando, FL 32862-0877

ISBN 1-56399-191-8

© 2002, Bill Bright. All rights reserved. No part of this book may be reproduced, stored in a retrieval system, or transmitted in any form or by any means, except in the case of brief quotations printed in articles or reviews, without prior permission in writing from the publisher.

Design and production by Genesis Group

Cover design by Koechel Peterson & Associates, Inc., Minneapolis, MN

Printed in the United States of America

Unless otherwise indicated, Scripture quotations are from the *New Living Translation*, © 1996 by Tyndale House Charitable Trust.

Scripture quotations designated NIV are from the *New International Version*, © 1973, 1978, 1984 by the International Bible Society. Published by Zondervan Bible Publishers, Grand Rapids, Michigan.

Scripture quotations designated TLB are from *The Living Bible*, © 1971 by Tyndale House Publishers, Wheaton, Illinois.

Contents

Acknowledgments 5

Introduction 7

CHAPTER 1: The Common Caller 11

CHAPTER 2: Two Kingdoms 19

CHAPTER 3: Hell 29

CHAPTER 4: Heaven 51

APPENDIX A: *Would You Like to Know God Personally?* 71

APPENDIX B: *The Spirit-filled Life* 81

End Notes 89

Resources 91

Acknowledgments

GOD HAS USED many people through the years to enhance my understanding of the truths that I have tried to communicate in this book. I am grateful for each of them. I especially want to thank Mike Richardson, whose research and editorial assistance were invaluable to the creation of this book, and John Barber and Tammy Campbell for their substantive editing. I appreciate Helmut Teichert for his creative input and oversight of this project. I also want to thank the other team members for their significant contributions: Nancy Schraeder and Lynn Copeland for help with editing; John Nill, publisher; and Michelle Treiber, cover coordinator and print broker.

Without a doubt, this book has challenged me as no other. It includes my admission that I have not given as much attention to the subjects involved as did our Lord and Savior Jesus Christ. I am grateful every moment to my Creator God and heavenly Father for He has rescued me from the kingdom of darkness and brought me into the kingdom of His dear Son, who purchased my freedom with His blood and has forgiven all my sins.

Of course my precious wife, Vonette, is a constant source of love and inspiration to me, and deserves special credit for her extra encouragement while I was involved in this book project amid more than one health crisis.

Introduction

LIFE IS FULL of choices. Which profession shall I pursue? Who should I marry? Where will I live? At some point in our lives, we all face these and a myriad of similar questions. Which of life's decisions are you facing? Are you seeking the best college? Deciding on a new car? Planning where you should take your next vacation? My sincere prayer is that you make the right choice.

Making the *right* choice in life is what this book is all about. But unlike the temporal choices represented in the above questions, this book focuses on *the* most important choice you face: a choice of heaven or hell. While the decisions that are part of daily living cannot be overlooked, our tendency is to become so preoccupied with such details that they obscure the more important questions bearing eternal weight. This is why it is so vitally important for you to stop now to consider where you want to spend eternity after you die. Are you willing to do this? My deep desire, dear reader, is to help you make this choice—the right choice—a choice that will enable you to experience a bit of heaven here on earth and the glory of heaven for all eternity.

Why do I share this message with you? Since I became a believer in 1945, I daily experience God's love and mercy. I know His forgiveness and fruitfulness, and I am awed at His faithfulness. I am confident that He has prepared a place for me in heaven. How can I know and experience these wonderful blessings and not share them with you?

Additionally, I share this vital word with you because Jesus said that He came to seek and save the lost. He spoke often about heaven and hell and the need for all to "repent, for the kingdom of heaven is near" (Matthew 4:17, NIV). Jesus preached this message because He cared about people. He longed for them to receive forgiveness of their sins, to be reconciled to their heavenly Father, and to have the gift of eternal life. Because Jesus lives inside me, His concern for others must be my concern. His message must be my message.

What specifically do I wish this book to accomplish in your life? First, if you are not trusting in Jesus Christ as your Lord and Savior, I pray that it will afford you a time of serious reflection on the essential matters of life and death, heaven and hell, which affect us all. Second, it will provide you with

Introduction

convincing information on the realities of heaven and hell that will assist you in reaching the most important decision of your life. Third, I pray that by the end of your reading you will take action, making the wise choice for heaven.

If you are a Christian, my aspiration for you is somewhat different. For you, my great desire is that this book will help *awaken* you to the spiritual condition of the world that is lost in sin and headed for hell—a place of unfathomable suffering, loss, and anguish. And that from this perspective, you will see afresh God's patience with sinful man in offering a way of escape from hell and its ravages through the merits of the gospel. This present hour is your opportunity to share Christ with others. Time is short. People all around you are in need of the knowledge you possess. Let this book rekindle your thirst for souls.

Regardless of who you are, please read this book prayerfully. Then, led by God's Spirit, share its message with others, helping to reach the world with the forgiveness and love of our great God and Savior. I dedicate this book to you, dear reader, with the earnest prayer that many millions of readers around the world will come to know Jesus personally, and that they will know without question the assurance of eternal life that comes only through Him.

CHAPTER 1

The Common Caller

SEPTEMBER 11, 2001, began as any other day. Spouses kissed each other good-bye before rushing out the door; children bustled off to school; workers checked their daily schedules as they commuted into the city. Tragically, at 8:48 a.m. life was never to be the same again. Two huge commercial airplanes, each guided by terrorists and loaded with 8,000 gallons of combustible jet fuel, exploded into the twin towers of the World Trade Center in New York City. Within minutes, a third jetliner guided by terrorists crashed into the Pentagon. A fourth plane crashed into a Pennsylvania field after heroic passengers stormed the hijackers, preventing what could have been an attack on the White House or our nation's capital.

Smoke and dust billowed from the intense fires of the collapsed towers. One firefighter likened the sight to "the gates of hell." The stench of death singed the nostrils of the brave emergency workers who selflessly walked into the inferno and rubble to try to save the victims. Television cameras recorded these tragic events for the world to see.

Approximately 3,000 people perished on September 11th. The rich died along with the poor, the famous with the unknown. Death, the great equalizer, had come calling.

Mourning, funerals, and eternity were unavoidable issues facing America, the wealthiest society in modern civilization. But all the gold and silver in the world was worth nothing to those who died, nor could any wealth bring back a lost loved one. Ironically, a quarter-billion dollars in gold and silver lay uselessly in the basement of the World Trade Center.

Crucial Questions

What became of those who died in the tragedy? Do they still exist outside their bodies? Did some go to heaven, as they had hoped? Did others go to hell? Did any go to a "holding pen" for eternal detainees awaiting final determination? Is there life after death? What is the ultimate end of life? At some point, everyone faces these and similar questions.

Every person who has ever lived shares a common experience: we each will die. Are you ready for eternity? "What profit is there if you gain the whole world—and lose eternal life?" (Matthew 16:26, TLB). That question was asked by the greatest Per-

The Common Caller

son of all time, Jesus of Nazareth.

But perhaps you question the reality of heaven and hell. The fact is that God's Word, the Bible, is proven to be history's most reliable document. It is replete with references to heaven and hell as real places where real people go at the end of their lives (John 14:2,3; Matthew 5:22; 18:8).

While the Bible alone contains God's personal message to us, some notion of heaven and hell is also found among many of the world's major religions, including Islam. Descriptions of heaven and hell vary from religion to religion; however, all agree that our position in the afterlife is determined by the choices we make in this life. It is not by chance that so many religions of the world mirror God's distinctive biblical teaching on life after death. Scripture says, "He has planted eternity in the human heart" (Ecclesiastes 3:11). Because all people have been created in the image of God, a deep awareness of eternity abides in the hearts of humankind. Nevertheless, only the Bible provides God's instruction on how to receive the gift of eternal life in heaven.

First Soundings

The first remembrance I have of "heaven" is from the lips of my godly mother. She was known as a

HEAVEN OR HELL

caring, serving, loving woman in the small community where I grew up on a ranch. And she often spoke of heaven as easily as she spoke of the grocery store or the bank. It was a definite place to her, and I mentally filed away her certainty about it.

As a youth, I heard churchgoers sing hymns such as "Heavenly Sunshine" and "When We All Get To Heaven." People testified about their joy in someday going to that "sweet by and by." Others talked about "heavenly" things—a heavenly gown, a heavenly dinner party, heavenly singing, and even heavenly good times of fellowship.

It is the joys of heaven that I so desperately want you to know and experience.

Then one day the pastor of our small church ran off with a woman, leaving his wonderful wife and family behind. Consequently, I decided there was not much that was heavenly in the church. Indeed, I decided heaven was what money could buy on earth, and I set my sights for what seemed like heaven to me—Hollywood, California. As a businessman, I worked hard and enjoyed material success, but deep in my heart I longed for "something more."

In 1945, through my mother's prayers and the ministry of the Hollywood First Presbyterian Church, I came to know the Maker of heaven and earth, our peerless, incomparable Savior, Jesus Christ. Knowing personally the Creator of the universe had rekindled my interest in heaven. After all, if He could create more than 100 billion galaxies like the Milky Way, then His ability to make a special place of indescribable beauty like heaven was no major accomplishment to Him, and not the least difficult for me to accept.

Since that time, I have believed that heaven awaits me. Following Jesus all these years has brought me to a vantage point where I can see down two corridors of time, each very clearly marked—one leading to heaven and its joy, the other leading to hell and its anguish. It is the joys of heaven that I so desperately want you to know and experience.

MEETING THE REALITY

In 1990, my urologist told me I had prostate cancer. In 1998, I was informed that I had an incurable disease, pulmonary fibrosis. In 2001, my blood tests confirmed the early stages of diabetes.

Over the years, as I have sat in the waiting rooms of hospitals and physician's offices, I have glanced around the room at those who waited with me. Their thoughts were written plainly on their faces: "What will I do if the news is bad?" Taut faces, pursed lips, nervous hands, darting eyes—all were indications that even the anticipation of bad news tortures us.

During those times, I have wanted to jump to my feet and tell each person of the joy I feel in knowing that death for me is merely a portal, a passage from this life to a much better one. In one breath I will pass from life to death to heaven, as will all who have received Jesus as Lord and Savior.

With gratitude to our great God and Savior, who has the final word in these matters, I can say that my incurable disease has given me a new and fresh walk with our Lord. I have been liberated to focus on some of the most important and exciting projects of my entire life.

Dear friend, I earnestly want to share with you the joyful assurance that you can have as you face the appointments of life and death. There is good news! We can walk in confidence, not in fear; in joyful expectation of a warm embrace from our loving God and Savior, not in dread of fiendish torment. With our eternity secure, we can be prepared for any sudden turn in the road of life. And we can help others get ready, too.

MAKING CHOICES

Are you willing to make a choice for either heaven or hell? It is so easy to do nothing about our spiritual lives. But "doing nothing" actually is making a

The Common Caller

choice. Someone has said, "Failing to plan is planning to fail." Sadly, when we choose to forestall a decision about where we stand with God, it is a decision that dishonors Him, and will ultimately result in our own destruction.

It breaks my heart to see people throwing their lives away, thoughtlessly, as if there were no tomorrow. If I could, I would wrap my arms around every person and tell them, "I love you too much *not* to tell you that God loves you. I love you too much *not* to ask you to please, stop and think about the tomorrows of your life and your eternal destiny." Today I plead with you to stop and think about the consequences of the choices you make. Consider your life and where you are headed. I beg you to consider what God thinks of your life, your footsteps, and your choices.

UNINFORMED CHOICE-MAKERS

I still mourn and weep over those who do not understand the reality of heaven and the wonderful Savior who has prepared it all for them. I grieve over those who have chosen to go their own selfish way, rejecting God's patience and His gracious offer of forgiveness in Christ. Thankfully for those who are still lost in their sins, Scripture teaches that there is time for them to repent and to receive the priceless gift of eternal life, bought and paid for on the cross by the blood of Jesus. Peter writes that God "does not want anyone to perish, so He is giving more time for everyone to repent" (2 Peter 3:9).

It is absolutely shocking and sad that so many people wander through life without certain knowledge of where they will spend their eternity. Through the years, Campus Crusade for Christ has taken many thousands of opinion surveys to learn where the culture has taken people in their thoughts and conduct. I was overwhelmed to tears to learn that nearly 95 percent of the thousands of students surveyed did not know for sure how to get to heaven. That is heartbreaking.

Even now, this is life's most crucial question: When you die and stand before God and He asks, "Why should I let you into My heaven?" what will your answer be?

CHAPTER 2

Two Kingdoms

LIFE FLOURISHES in contrasts. The sweetest smelling crimson rose grows on a plain, thorny stem. The brightest full moon shines best in the darkest night. The glory and goodness of heaven has a dark opposite. I shall never forget my adventure into light and darkness during a tour of a massive underground cave. The guide took us deeper and deeper into the darker and darker labyrinth. Then he stopped and gave us a warning: "The lights are going out. Stand still; you'll be all right. We will experience total darkness for a minute and then turn the lights back on."

Well, "a minute" seemed like an eternity. When the lights went out, the darkness seemed suffocating. I did not know where I was. I could not see anyone. I could barely sense the breathing and shuffling of those near me. "Listen to the quiet," the guide said. I was glad to know he was still there. I am sure that not more than 20 seconds went by before someone shouted, "Turn on the lights!" The fellow had given voice to my heart's cry, too. I shall never forget how dark it was in that underground cave.

Two Destinies, Two Destinations

The contrast between light and dark in creation mirrors the spiritual contrasts that have existed for ages. The Bible says there are only two kingdoms: the kingdom of light and the kingdom of darkness. God's kingdom of light is one of perfect peace, bliss, and joy. It is where God dwells in all His fullness and where His children enjoy life abundant and eternal.

The other kingdom—the kingdom of darkness—belongs to Satan,[1] who was once known as Lucifer. Lucifer was created by God as an angel of light, but he rebelled by seeking equality with God (Isaiah 14:12–14). One-third of heaven's angelic forces rebelled with Lucifer. Before we become children of God, we live in the kingdom of darkness.

Although there are two kingdoms, they are not equal. Satan operates with a limited, "derived" authority. He can do nothing apart from the sovereign power and permission of Almighty God. The enemy of our souls has no power to harm or hinder us except as God may allow (as He did in the life of Job). One day God will withdraw His permission. Thus, Satan is only *temporarily* the "prince of the power of the air" (Ephesians 2:2). He has dominion over

Two Kingdoms

his demonic forces, but unlike God, he is not all-knowing, ever-present, or all-powerful.

Satan does not know our thoughts and he cannot possess a Christian. Where the Holy Spirit is in control, the evil one is completely powerless. "The Spirit who lives in you is greater than the spirit who lives in the world" (1 John 4:4).

Because the kingdoms of light and darkness are spiritual in nature, they cannot be reduced to specific locations. Nonetheless, they do contain unambiguous places where people will spend eternity, depending on their acceptance or rejection of Christ. These two places are heaven (part of the kingdom of light) and hell (part of the kingdom of darkness). In the next two chapters, we will take a detailed look at these two destinations, heaven and hell. But first, let us look briefly at the two spiritual kingdoms, beginning with where every person starts—in the dark.

KINGDOM OF DARKNESS

One of Satan's names, the "devil," comes from the Greek word *diabolos*, which means "slanderer." He is the father of lies and the accuser of all mankind. Lies, accusations, distortions, and half-truths characterize his dark kingdom. The devil's goals, according to Jesus, are to steal, kill, and destroy (John 10:10). This includes robbing us of the joy of our salvation and encouraging the kingdom of darkness to harm us through theft, murder, stolen virtue, broken homes, and broken hearts. It is not a pretty kingdom in its purposes or its tactics, but it has a certain appeal. The Bible says, "Men loved darkness instead of light because their deeds were evil" (John 3:19, NIV). Our society knows all too well that crime is more likely to occur at night. The more light there is, the less crime there will be.

At the same time, urban centers such as Las Vegas, Nevada, are ablaze at night with lights, while much of what goes on there—drinking alcohol, gambling, sexual immorality—is definitely rooted in the kingdom of darkness. The devil uses the world system to tantalize mankind with fame, fortune, pleasure, and power. He draws people away from God in an underhanded way—not by dressing up in a red suit and leading a parade, but by coyly and shrewdly undermining our faith and obedience toward God and our love and kindness toward humanity. It is not a pleasant thought to realize that before we become followers of Jesus we are all subjects of Satan's kingdom (Ephesians 2:2).

With followers of Christ, Satan uses doubt, distraction, and discouragement. He mocks and usurps authority. Those under his influence do the same. He is frustrated that God is the ultimate authority.

He knows he is a defeated foe, subject to eternal punishment, and he is out to take as many men, women, and children as possible down to hell with him. He loves to belittle followers of Jesus by making accusations against them. Martin Luther, whose ministry sparked the Reformation of the Church, found his mind constantly being attacked by satanic accusations of failure, sin, omissions, and commissions. In agony, Luther confronted the evil one and claimed the promise of 1 John 1:7: "The blood of Jesus Christ... cleanses us from all sin."

In confrontations with the enemy, we would do well to follow the counsel of renowned pastor and theologian Martyn Lloyd-Jones: "Never look back at your sins again. Say: 'It is finished, it is answered by the Blood of Christ.' That is your first step."[2] Amen!

KINGDOM OF LIGHT

The terms "kingdom of heaven" and "kingdom of God" are synonymous with the "kingdom of light" (see Matthew 4:17; Mark 1:15; Colossians 1:12,13). The central feature of God's kingdom is His unique kingship, or rule, from heaven. Because God is eternal, His kingdom is also eternal. His kingdom is not physical. Rather, it is a spiritual kingdom, where all the spiritual blessings and possessions of God exist perfectly without change. Every man, woman, and child becomes an heir to all that is part of the kingdom of light the moment they trust in Christ for the forgiveness of their sins. Thus, in this life, believers know God's blessings only in part. But when the believer dies, God brings him or her to a specific location called heaven where all the blessings of God are known fully.

The kingdom of light is interesting in that it contains past, present, and future aspects. Prophets of old foretold the kingdom of God (Zechariah 9:9; Daniel 2:44). The kingdom is present in believers (Matthew 6:10; Luke 17:21). And the fullness of the kingdom will come in power when Christ comes again (Matthew 16:28; Mark 8:38–9:1).

Other important facts about the kingdom include: repentance and faith bring us into the kingdom (Matthew 4:17); seeking the kingdom should be our highest priority (Matthew 13:44); the new birth supplies entrance to the kingdom (John 3:5); and throughout the Bible, the purpose of the kingdom of heaven is to glorify God (Daniel 7:14).

Choosing Sides

When President George W. Bush faced the world to speak of the evildoers who wreaked death and destruction on New York City and Washington on September 11, 2001, he issued this challenge: "Every

Two Kingdoms

country in every region has a decision to make: You are either with us, or you're with the terrorists." Later, he pointedly added that those who aided and abetted the terrorists would "share the same fate" as the terrorists.

These statements are exact parallels of the choices God has offered humanity. We either accept Christ, choosing to stand with Him in the kingdom of light, or we reject Christ, choosing to stand with the devil and his angels in history's final hour of judgment. "No one can serve two masters," Jesus said (Matthew 6:24). Elsewhere He declared, "He who is not with Me is against Me" (Matthew 12:30, NIV). Thus, it is imperative that we heed the call of Joshua, who declared under the inspiration of the Holy Spirit, "Choose today whom you will serve" (Joshua 24:15).

> *There rages a war between good and evil, and each day we choose on which side we stand.*

The horrible events of September 11th reawakened many Americans to the harsh reality that there are forces of evil in this world, that there rages a war between good and evil, and each day we choose on which side we stand.

President Abraham Lincoln was asked during the Civil War if God was on the side of the Union.

Lincoln replied that the larger question was whether the Union was on God's side. Are you on God's side today?

Once I was invited to speak to a luncheon gathering of U.S. Senators in Washington, D.C. Such affairs are rare in religious circles. In fact, it seemed a miracle that 26 members of the "most powerful club in the world," as it has become known, would actually show up to hear me speak. From my view, they came largely in deference to one of their colleagues, Senator Bill Armstrong, who had invited them. When I walked into the room, I was pretty sure God had made a mistake! Gathered here were some of the most politically liberal and most politically conservative of men—two opposite ends of the spectrum. How could I possibly appeal to both sides?

> *We are either light dispelling darkness or we are wallowing in the deadly darkness of sin.*

The Lord had given me what appeared to be the oddest message for that gathering: two kingdoms, darkness and light, heaven and hell. I thought, *Lord, are You sure?* The topic did not seem appropriate given the culture and refinement of the occasion. I was thinking I should say something more socially relevant to such a prestigious group, but He made it clear this was what He want-

Two Kingdoms

ed me to share. This was the choice all must make, whether rich and powerful or poor and weak: In whose kingdom are you?

I shared the Good News that God "has rescued us out of the darkness and gloom of Satan's kingdom and brought us into the kingdom of His dear Son, who bought our freedom with His blood and forgave us all our sins" (Colossians 1:13,14, TLB). Although the full impact of these words was not apparent at the time, I trust that perhaps some of those Senators responded to His message of "two kingdoms."

Despite all the choices and philosophies strewn about the landscape of our time, there remain only two kingdoms: the kingdom of light and the kingdom of darkness—the kingdom of God and the realms dominated by Satan. Ultimately, we all decide whether to walk in the light or in the darkness. There are no half-lit Christians. We are either light dispelling darkness or we are wallowing in the deadly darkness of sin. Like Paul, we must celebrate, for our sake and the glory of God, that He has delivered us from the power of darkness into His kingdom.

Now that we have looked at the two kingdoms, we will begin in the next chapter to look at the ultimate resting place for the members of each kingdom—heaven or hell. This book is not intended to provide a scholarly treatise on these subjects. Others who prefer that approach have done that. Rather, I want to emphasize our personal relationship with God the Father through the Lord Jesus. The fact is that the history of biblical interpretation has different camps. One emphasizes a literal understanding of what Scripture says about heaven and hell, with dates and numbers viewed as actual. The other emphasizes poetic understanding, viewing words as symbols more often than not. Both believe the Bible is declaring God's truth, but they differ in the use of literal terms. I do not wish to take sides in this debate, but have drawn heavily from both camps in order to underscore the urgent need for people everywhere to choose heaven over hell.

CHAPTER 3

Hell

IS THERE REALLY a hell? Is it a rowdy tavern kept by a fellow in a red suit with horns and a tail? If not, what is it like? Every day, people tell others to go there. They laugh at how their conduct here will be only slightly changed there. Declaring their delight in sin and disdain for the Savior, some have said they would "rather rule in hell than serve in heaven."

Who can be comfortable describing hell? Yet there is no way I can deny the truth of hell's existence. Jesus made it a priority to warn of hell and to advise how to avoid it, so how can His followers be silent? I agree with the famous evangelist D. L. Moody, founder of Chicago's Moody Church and the Moody Bible Institute, who said, "When we preach on hell, we might at least do it with tears in our eyes."[3]

Every day we hear people equate their worst feelings with hell. Emergency personnel describe the smell of burning flesh at an accident scene as "something out of hell." Hollywood movies depict the bitter and nauseating tastes of hell. It is portrayed as a painful place where tortured voices fill the head with screams and pleas for help. Satan is viewed as laughing at the fate of those who traded their souls with him for profit and fame but found him false. He seems to jeer, "You bought the lie! You bought the lie!" As theologian Wayne Grudem puts it, "The devil's characteristic has been to originate sin and tempt others to sin," and that sin, without Christ's saving grace, will cause us to be residents of hell.[4]

Jonathan Edwards, famous revivalist of the Great Awakening of the 18th century, preached about the horrors of hell:

> To help your conception, imagine yourself to be cast into a fiery oven, all of a glowing heat, or into the midst of a glowing brick kiln, or of a great furnace, where your pain would be as much greater than that occasioned by accidentally touching a coal of fire, as the heat is greater. Imagine also that your body were to lie there for a quarter of an hour, full of fire, as full within and without as a bright coal of fire, all the while full of quick sense; what horror would you feel at the entrance of such a furnace! And how long would that quarter of an hour seem to you!

...And how much greater would be the effect, if you knew you must endure it for a whole year, and how vastly greater still, if you knew you must endure it for a thousand years! O then, how would your heart sink, if you thought, if you knew, that you must bear it forever and ever!...That after millions of millions of ages, your torment would be no nearer to an end, than ever it was; and that you never, never should be delivered! But your torment in Hell will be immeasurably greater than this illustration represents.[5]

This passage paints a grim picture of what hell is like. Is that really the way it will be?

HELL AND THE BIBLE

Scripture has much to say in describing hell. Here is a summary of a few elements of hell:

Hell is a place of punishment for those who do not know God personally. Jesus said, "If your hand or your foot causes you to sin, cut it off and throw it away. It is better for you to enter life maimed or crippled than to have two hands or two feet and be thrown into eternal fire" (Matthew 18:8, NIV). Clearly, hell is a place of unquenchable fire (Matthew 3:12), and it is eternal (Mark 9:48). It is a place of utter torment (Revelation 14:10,11) and outer darkness

(Matthew 8:12; 22:13).

The word "hell" is translated from "Gehenna," a narrow valley outside Jerusalem where idolaters burned their children as sacrifices to the god Molech. It later became the city's stinking, ever-burning garbage dump. As the place where the bodies of dead animals and criminals were thrown into the continuous fire, it came to picture everlasting destruction. This was the analogy Jesus used to describe hell as eternal torment.

In His approximately 42 months of public ministry, there are 33 recorded instances of Jesus speaking about hell. No doubt he warned of hell thousands of times. The Bible refers to hell a total of 167 times.

> *Jesus spent more time warning of the impending judgment of hell than speaking of the joys of heaven.*

I wonder with what frequency this eternal subject is found in today's pulpits. I confess I have failed in my ministry to declare the reality of hell as often as I have the love of God and the benefits of a personal relationship with Christ. But Jesus spent more of His time warning His listeners of the impending judgment of hell than speaking of the joys of heaven. God never planned for any human ever to go to hell. It has never been my emphasis to focus on hell because it is a place designed by God for our

Hell

enemy and his demons. Jesus said hell was "The eternal fire prepared for the devil and his demons" (Matthew 25:41). Yet all who insist on following Satan here on earth, by living sinful, disobedient lives, must be prepared to spend eternity with him in hell. Never forget, there is a cross at the entrance to hell. The only way man can go there is to push the cross aside and deliberately reject God's love and forgiveness.

Jesus describes the place of final and eternal punishment as the "lake of fire" (Revelation 20:14, 15). God did not establish hell for the purpose of scaring people into heaven. But it is a biblical fact that a place of eternal punishment exists, and those who do not know Jesus as their personal Savior ignore it to their own destruction.

Hell is a real place that will shatter many people's delusions about the afterlife. There are many misconceptions about the reality of hell. One is the idea that a loving God, by His nature, would not send anyone to such an awful place. Another is the concept of reincarnation—we die only to come to life again as a different creature. Others believe that, after the body dies, the soul is absorbed into the cosmos or is dissolved into a supreme being. In either case, the individual personality ceases to exist. Many people believe that hell will be fun—not a place of torment or punishment, but merely a moral cesspool where they will spend eternity with their friends.

Other theories include soul sleep, in which the soul merely goes to sleep and exists in that state forever, and purgatory, an "in-between" location of punishment from which one may be delivered after being prayed for or even paid for through monetary offerings! Last is the often-quoted notion that "hell is on earth."

Although these are widely held ideas in the court of public opinion, the significance of one "expert witness" cannot be overlooked. Paul tells us that after Jesus' death, He descended into hell (Ephesians 4:9). Peter agrees but goes further stating that Jesus actually preached to the dead in hell (1 Peter 4:6). Obviously, Jesus of Nazareth can speak credibly about time and eternity as He alone has first-hand knowledge about hell.

How did Jesus describe hell? On one occasion, He told of a certain rich man who died and went to a hellish place. Many believe this was no parable because unlike any parable of Christ, the primary figure refers to specific people: Abraham and Lazarus. We need only read Luke 16:19–31. There we will see the words of Jesus of Nazareth, the Son of God, the most credible Person in all history. He not only details the agony and suffering of a person aware of the fierce torment all around him, but shows that this person is aware of others on earth who are delaying their decision to avoid hell. The fire and heat are so great and unquenchable that the rich man begs Lazarus for simply a drop of water!

Jesus also spoke of the "fires of hell" (Matthew 5:22) and the "fiery furnace" (Matthew 13:42, NIV). Jesus used the purging power of fire to convey God's holiness against evil and sin, as well as His punishment by inflicting suffering.

Hell is a place where God sends unrepentant sinners. I am often asked, "How can a loving God send anyone to hell?" This question betrays an incorrect understanding of God. Although God is loving and merciful, He is also holy, righteous, and just. To emphasize some of His attributes at the expense of others creates a distorted view of who God is and therefore creates false expectations of what He will do at the judgment seat.

As I read the Bible, I read of a God of love and compassion who created men and women in His own image and made available to us a wonderful life of beauty—rich and full of His presence and provision. But I also read of a God who is holy. Therefore, He has provided us with His Ten Commandments (Exodus 20:3–17) and the Golden Rule

(Matthew 7:12) to establish a standard of holiness for our lives.

In the Ten Commandments, we can clearly understand our sinfulness and our need for His grace. God commands:

    I. Do not worship any other gods besides Me.
    II. Do not make idols of any kind.
    III. Do not misuse the name of the LORD your God.
    IV. Remember to observe the Sabbath day by keeping it holy.
    V. Honor your father and mother.
    VI. Do not murder.
    VII. Do not commit adultery.
    VIII. Do not steal.
    IX. Do not testify falsely against your neighbor.
    X. Do not covet.

How many of these have you broken? The Bible says that to offend God in breaking one of these is to have broken all of them! The truth is that everyone has broken God's perfect Law. We have each lied, or looked at a person lustfully, or coveted someone else's property. Who, then, can stand before a holy God?

Because God is holy, He cannot, will not, allow sin in His presence. The Bible tells us that His "eyes are too pure to look on evil" (Habakkuk 1:13, NIV) and that He "cannot tolerate the slightest sin" (Psalm 5:4). Because He is also just, He cannot let sin go unpunished. Breaking these commandments will take us to hell without the intervening grace and mercy of Jesus Christ.

When Christ died on the cross, He became the atoning sacrifice for our sins. Those who reject His atonement will stand in judgment when they die and will suffer God's punishment—eternity in hell.

Again, God did not create hell for humans, but for Satan and the rebellious angels who followed him. But our sins, left unforgiven, qualify us for no other destination. Committing a crime leads a criminal to be arrested and appear before a judge. When guilt is established, the judge is required by law to sentence the criminal to the proper punishment, often including prison. Similarly, our sins against God lead to our arrest and appearance before the Eternal Judge who one day will execute the sentence of eternal imprisonment as our just punishment (Revelation 20:15). Those who have trusted the Lord Jesus Christ have their sins forgiven and have Him as "one who speaks to the Father in our defense" (1 John 2:2).

As with individuals, nations too must heed the Bible's words. God always blesses the obedient and chastens the disobedient. Scripture records, "Blessed is the nation whose God is the Lord" (Psalm 33:12, NIV). Whether individuals or nations, when we ignore God's timeless standards (the Ten Commandments), indeed when we fail the two great commandments—"Love the Lord your God with all your heart and with all your soul and with all your mind... Love your neighbor as yourself" (Matthew 22:37–40, NIV)—we simply write the order for our eternal punishment by a holy God.

Hell is a place of unfathomable torture. To meditate on the Scriptures describing hell is to experience nightmares of a terrible reality. As I previously mentioned, Jesus speaks of hell as a place of unquenchable fire where "there will be weeping and gnashing of teeth" (Matthew 13:42). This torment by itself portrays a condition one would never want to experience. The teeth will grate from extreme frustration amid pain and rage. On this earth, we may know the pain of touching a hot stove or an overheated auto engine. We draw back, repulsed by the pain for a few moments. But imagine if those moments extended for a million billion years! It would be as if a volcano had erupted and we found ourselves swimming in the hot molten lava, alone, forever, with no hope of rescue or relief, ever.

All the senses will be under attack. Our nostrils will burn with stinging heat, and we will smell the

Hell

stench of burning flesh. We will taste our own vomit. We will hear the wails of others whom we cannot see, and consequently, we will not be able to aid them. We will see only the unending nature of this torment; although there will be unimaginable heat, there will be no light in this tunnel of eternal darkness. Every touch will cause the flesh to rot and fall away, and we won't be able to bring one moment's comfort to our bodies (Matthew 18:8; 22:13).

In hell the body will be in such intense pain that it will seem almost paralyzed. The inner person will burn with anger—at self, at God, at the devil, at others. This anger will flood the soul with pain. Constant turmoil will dominate the mind, and there will be no time-out, no "do-over," no respite, no relief, no place of appeal, no friend to turn to, no way out, no light, no ending of it, no lessening of it, no prospect nor hope of it ever coming to pass. It will stay, nag, burn, churn the stomach, grimace the soul. It will bring regret and tragic sensations of abject failure, lost opportunity, and utter hopelessness.

Worse yet will be the utter loss of control—a sense of falling with no ability to correct the course or sense any landing place. We will be eternally sinking, fearing, with no points of reference, no lighthouses, no directional signs, no buttons to push, no wheel to steer, no commands to give and no one to answer, no control! Forever! Always! Torment without end!

The Bible says that "the demons believe...and they tremble in terror" (James 2:19). The word used for "tremble" means to bristle in fearful sensation, a physical response—like the first time you entered a "haunted house." How many of us have been walking alone at night when something suddenly stirs, and a cat shrieks that sucking, semi-hissing sound? We react as we would to fingernails on a chalkboard—our body tenses, chills go up and down our spine—and we are scared witless! That is only the tiniest tinge of the trembling, flinching, fear-filled anticipation that will be the diet of every person in hell. John Wesley, Oxford scholar and founder of the Methodist church, explained, "Fierce and poisonous animals were created for terrifying man, in order that he might be made aware of the final judgment in hell."[6]

Hell is a place under God's control. Decades ago, my own reflection was that the worst thing about hell would be *the absence* of the presence of our loving Creator, the Lord God (2 Thessalonians 1:9). Not to walk with Him nor know the joy of His presence would be hellish enough for me. But the Bible reveals something much worse: it declares our God is present everywhere, even in hell! David states, "I

Hell

can never escape from Your Spirit! I can never get away from Your presence! If I go up to heaven, You are there; if I go down to the place of the dead, You are there" (Psalm 139:7,8). What is His presence in hell accomplishing? The enforcement of His eternal punishment through wrath. Many have the misconception that the devil is in charge of hell. Not true! God is always in charge!

Though I have known the love and grace of our merciful God since 1945, I also know what the Bible teaches about the justice and wrath of God. As a result, I have a holy fear and reverence for God and am far more concerned about what He thinks of me and my conduct than the opinions of all of earth's inhabitants combined. "Don't be afraid of those who can kill only your bodies—but can't touch your souls! Fear only God who can destroy both soul and body in hell" (Matthew 10:28, TLB).

Hell is a place that lasts forever. At the close of the 1980s, there arose in America the notion that not all people are born immortal. God gifts only certain people with immortality and, consequently, those who have not received Christ may not be subject to eternal punishment in hell. This theory, called conditional immortality, is a dangerous departure from the Bible's clear teaching.

Another theory, called annihilationism, teaches

that man was created immortal, but that God does not send those who reject Christ to an eternal hell. Instead, He merely deprives them of immortality whereby they simply cease to exist.

Although I respect those who take these questionable positions, I must declare without reservation that hell is a real and eternal place for all who fail to claim God's forgiveness. Hell, according to Jesus, is a place of torment, anguish, flames, personal loss, and mental awareness for an "everlasting" period. It is unbearable agony—forever.

> *Hell is a real and eternal place for all who fail to claim God's forgiveness.*

The concept of eventual annihilation "seriously underestimates the pains of hell; indeed, the lost would rather be annihilated because their suffering would be over," observes Robert A. Peterson, professor of systematic theology at Covenant Theological Seminary in St. Louis.[7]

Those who hold the traditional view of a literal, eternal hell include some of the greatest scholars and theologians since the time of Christ, as well as tens of thousands of contemporary pastors, scholars, and theologians. I join them in standing with the clear teaching of our Lord Jesus Christ and the apostle Paul.

My understanding of the nature of God is that

Hell

He deals in eternal rewards and eternal consequences. God will not suddenly turn off the punishment. If that were so, I believe Jesus would have wanted us all to know it quite specifically, from His own lips. The record, however, is that everything He said on the subject points to the contrary. He tells us that the wicked "will go away into eternal punishment, but the righteous will go into eternal life" (Matthew 25:46). We are created as immortal beings, and hell lasts forever.

NEGLECTING OUR DUTY

It is the duty of every believer to warn others of the reality of hell. Permit me to illustrate with a brief story. As ships were crossing the channel for the invasion of Europe on D-Day, June 6, 1944, a young soldier asked a chaplain if he believed in hell. The chaplain said that he did *not* believe in hell! An officer overheard the chaplain's reply and demanded to know why he didn't resign his commission immediately.

"Why should I?" the chaplain asked.

The officer snapped, "Because if there is no such place as hell, we don't need you, and if there is, we don't need to be lied to at a time such as this."

Our world cannot afford to be lied to about such a crucial issue as hell. Every believer must see this present hour as a God-sent opportunity to warn the lost of the dangers of hell. We stand in the formidable company of great scholars and theologians when we accept the reality of hell.

"Hell is truth seen too late," stated Thomas Hobbes.[8]

Billy Graham said, "Unless we believe in a future judgment or that people are lost forever without Christ, the cutting edge of evangelism is blunted."[9]

G. Campbell Morgan, a 19th century preacher of renown, said, "I am bound to admit that I have seen a far larger number surrender to Christ when I have been preaching on the terrible results of neglecting salvation than when dwelling on any other theme."[10]

And J. C. Ryle added, "The watchman who keeps silent when he sees a fire is guilty of gross neglect. The doctor who tells us we are getting well when we are dying is a false friend, and the minister who keeps back hell from his people in his sermons is neither a faithful nor a charitable man."[11]

Therefore, we should be like the prophet Ezekiel, the "watchman on the wall," telling our society, family, friends, and neighbors of the reality of heaven and hell. We are to be engaged in "snatching them from the flames of judgment" (Jude 23). This act simply requires caring enough to warn of the

Hell

very real danger of living without Christ. We need only tell people the truth: There is a hell to shun and a heaven to gain. We must join the apostle Paul who declared, "It is because we know this solemn fear of the Lord that we work so hard to persuade others" (2 Corinthians 5:11).

It is our duty to share eternal truths with those we encounter. But what about their responsibility? Let's look at that now.

HEEDING THE WARNING

To some, it seemed to be just another Louisiana gullywasher, a typical after-dark downpour. Drivers approaching the great Lake Ponchatrain Bridge were taking the typical route into New Orleans, most returning home late. By nightfall the lake itself was heaving. Pouring rain, howling wind, and sudden flashes of lightning made the drivers think about the situation, not their souls. It was enough to focus on their destinations, not their destinies. For many years, the bridge had been the main way in and out of the famous city. But this night, the bridge was changed forever.

Massive flooding sucked pilings from under a portion of the bridge, and a long section washed away. In the darkness, a driver slammed on his brakes and realized how close he came to plunging into the raging waters. Others ahead of him had already plummeted into the flood and were drowning. As he got out of his car and looked back, he saw other cars coming. He ran toward them, waving his arms, screaming, "Stop! Please don't go on this way! The bridge is out! No! Stop! You must stop!"

He waved. He jumped. He shouted. He was nearly struck by an oncoming car as he confronted several drivers with the danger ahead. Some heeded his warnings. Others ignored him that fateful night, and they perished in the torrent en route to eternity.

I can only imagine what they had on their minds as they were speeding along—a pending business deal, the children, the grandchildren, making ends meet, planning some fun, worrying about a loved one.

How did those who fell into the river feel? They had no clue the bridge would collapse. How could they have known it would be their fate to fall into deadly waters? There is no driver training class for what to do when a bridge washes out. They were not prepared for how to respond. They must have been panic-stricken, trying to decide whether to ride out the raging river inside the car or to try to get out of the car, drowning being a strong risk with either option. What were they doing or thinking as the abyss was swallowing them? Did those who saw the man's

Hell

warning regret not heeding it? Where would this river take them? To death? And if so, where then?

Like most people, I have driven many miles, never expecting to meet with death. Shortly after Vonette and I were married, a freak accident very well could have cost us our lives. Just as we were passing a large semi-trailer truck, its front wheel came off and tore into the side of our new car. Only God spared our lives. Looking back, I realize I was like many people who are so busy that they never stop to think about the certain appointment we all have with death.

God spoke these words through the prophet Ezekiel, "As surely as I live, declares the Sovereign LORD, I take no pleasure in the death of the wicked, but rather that they turn from their ways and live. Turn! Turn from your evil ways!" (33:11, NIV).

Are you prepared for where you will spend eternity? Do not wait to answer this question until it's too late. You never know when a flood will wash away the bridges in your life. If you don't know Jesus Christ as your personal Savior, I urge you right now to take a few moments to turn to the back of this book and read Appendix A, "Would You Like to Know God Personally?" Then you can settle this most important issue of where you will spend eternity.

A Personal Perspective

For me, the knowledge of "the most joyful news ever announced"—the saving love of Jesus Christ—has always been enough motivation for me to seek to help fulfill His Great Commission. To take His message of love and forgiveness to every person on earth is so wonderful and so compelling, I have never felt the need to focus on telling people about hell.

However, as a result of a steady decline in morals and spiritual vitality in today's culture and a growing indifference to the afterlife, I have come to realize the need for a greater discussion of hell. Today we are seeing the reality of the kingdom of darkness in a sharp increase among avowed satanic cults, devil worshipers, and witch covens. *USA Today* reports that Wicca (witchcraft) is the fastest growing religion in America—growing at an astounding annual rate of more than 1,500 percent![12]

I have thus come to see that silence, or even benign neglect on these subjects, is disobedience on my part. To be silent on the eternal destinations of souls is to be like a sentry failing to warn his fellow soldiers of impending attack. It is like knowing calamity is coming and not sounding the alarm.

What is your eternal spiritual condition? What is the eternal destiny of your loved ones, co-workers,

Hell

and neighbors?

Today, I admonish you to "fear only God, who can destroy both soul and body in hell" (Matthew 10:28). That the Bible even mentions hell is one of the greatest proofs of God's love for you. If He didn't love you, there would be no warning of hell and no cross upon which Jesus died.

For those who accept the Lord Jesus as their Savior, the horrors of hell will no longer be their final destination. Instead, the redeemed can look forward to a magnificent place called heaven. But we must not go there without taking along as many people as we can. We must realize that our neighbors, loved ones, and friends who have not received Christ are going to spend eternity separated from the Lord. Every believer should be concerned for his or her unbelieving children and grandchildren, spouse, siblings, parents and grandparents. This is not a small issue. It is a matter of all eternity.

> *We must not go to heaven without taking along as many people as we can.*

As of this writing, I am finishing a forty-day fast with the prayer that God would send a revival of spiritual awakening so that more people will spend eternity in heaven. I have not denied my body the pleasures of food just to experience a religious ritual, but because of deep compassion and concern for the souls of those who are lost without Christ. I have been literally pleading for the souls of millions before the throne of grace.

Charles Spurgeon, the prince of preachers, pleaded with believers:

> If sinners be damned, at least let them leap to hell over our bodies. And if they will perish, let them perish with our arms about their knees, imploring them to stay. If hell must be filled, at least let it be filled in the teeth of our exertions, and let not one go there unwarned and unprayed for.

If you are timid about witnessing, or are letting a fear of man keep you from sharing the greatest news ever, please read Appendix B to learn how to have a Spirit-filled life of boldness. If you do not know how to witness about our Lord, I beg of you, contact my office and you can obtain material that will help you understand how to introduce loved ones to Christ.

Now, as we turn to the next chapter, we will look at the glories that await the believer in heaven.

CHAPTER 4

Heaven

WHAT IS THE best part of traveling? For me, after more than six decades of journeys, over many millions of miles, near and very far, the answer is still the same: The best part of a trip is coming "home." Countless times while traveling, I have been asked where I was from. Although I was born in Oklahoma in 1921, moved to California in 1944 and to Florida in 1991, I usually reply that I am from America, because I truly feel the whole nation is my home. Likewise for a Christian, though we have been born and reside in some state or nation, our ultimate home is in heaven. Every believer should long to be there.

Charles Spurgeon once prayed, "May we live here like strangers and make the world not a house, but an inn, in which we sup and lodge, expecting to be on our journey tomorrow."[13]

The song "Finally Home" describes it this way: "Just think of stepping on shore, and finding it heaven, of touching a hand and finding it God's, of breathing new air and finding it celestial, of waking up in glory and finding it home."[14]

Most of us do not fully apprehend the beauty and glory of heaven. Permit me to explore this place of unparalleled splendor and blessing with you.

WHAT IS HEAVEN LIKE?

I will begin my description of heaven with the observation that there are many things we simply do not know. Although the Bible is full of references to heaven, it leaves many questions unanswered. "As [Martin] Luther has said, we know as little about the next life as a baby in the womb knows about the life he is to enter," writes J. I. Packer. "But every believer knows this: in the gift of the Holy Spirit, God has given him a foretaste, the first fruits, the down payment of the powers of the world to come."[15]

I once prayed to our Savior and asked why Scripture lacked complete information about heaven. He impressed me that if we knew all about heaven while on earth, then we would be prone to fall in love with it, rather than with Him who created it. Thus, because Scripture is silent on many issues regarding heaven, I also must remain silent. Frankly, the mere thought of heaven is more than my finite mind can grasp. The following description of the believer's eternal home therefore represents but a fraction of all the joy, freedom, and blessings that God's children shall enjoy there. It is with great joy that I share these things with you now.

Heaven is a specific place promised and prepared by Jesus for those who follow Him. Jesus said, "Don't be troubled. You trust in God, now trust in Me. There are many rooms in my Father's home, and I am going to prepare a place for you. If this were not so, I would tell you plainly. When everything is ready, I will come and get you so that you will always be with Me where I am" (John 14:1–3).

God is always true to His Word. The Lord has gone, as He said He would, to "prepare a place for you." The King James version describes our future home in heaven as a "mansion." Because the modern world has so many physical mansions, we are inclined to envision that in heaven we will live in a sprawling house with a great view of a golf course and a lake. But such a view does heaven a great disservice. The mansion of which Jesus spoke can be described in more than physical terms. It will be a place of God's complete presence, where all loneliness, fear, and discouragement will be gone. We will know nothing but the presence of a totally satisfying assurance. Peace, in the fullest sense of the word, will be our common experience. Heaven will be a place of absolute satisfaction and contentment. There we will dwell with our God and Savior forever.

Heaven is a place of welcome. Heaven, I am confident, will *not* be a place where we must "check in" with St. Peter, as suggested by many jokes. Rather, heaven is our home, first of all, because the Father delights in welcoming us. We will receive greetings beyond measure; the intimacy of a hug from God the Father will be our first joy. Wrapped in His loving embrace we will sense peace, delight, assurance, great love, warm fellowship, total security, and absolute calm.

> Each true believer's name is recorded in heaven's registry, the Lamb's Book of Life.

Heaven is a place where Christ, our heavenly Bridegroom, meets His bride-to-be, the Church, the congregation of believers who have responded to His finished work (Hebrews 12:22,23; Revelation 19:7,8). Our joyous reception will not be based on any works of righteousness we did while on earth, but will be founded on the blood of the Savior shed for us (Ephesians 2:8,9; Titus 3:5). Because each true believer's name is recorded in heaven's registry, the Lamb's Book of Life, our reservations are forever sure (Luke 10:20; Revelation 21:27).

On the other hand, many people who die will

presume to have a welcome in heaven. They will say, "Lord, Lord, we told others about You and used Your name to cast out demons and to do many other great miracles." But Jesus will reply, "You have never been mine. Go away, for your deeds are evil" (Matthew 7:23, TLB). What a horrifying day that will be for countless people.

Heaven is a place of reunion and unity, where we will very likely see Christian loved ones. How joyous to be able to see once again our precious family and friends who have died and gone on before us. Truly, what a day that will be! The mere prospect of being reunited with loved ones and friends makes heaven a place of joy beyond comparison. Brought together in the exquisite, all-surrounding presence of the Lord, our faces will beam. Our countenances will gleam, and we will shout in such delight that angels will glance at each other in wonderment!

Also, we will experience absolutely no sense of inferiority or superiority. We are each complete in Christ (Colossians 2:10). Because we are in a glorified state, without sin, there will be no sense of prejudice between God's children. We will be a vast gathering of peoples from every part of earth with the full realization that we are all of equal standing in His eyes. We will love and accept each other because we have been loved unconditionally and accepted by our common Savior, the Lord Jesus Christ.

No face is veiled, no head covered. We all will be of the same heavenly class. We will be a sea of happy faces—a holy bliss! No joyous concert on earth could hold a candle to the energy, enthusiasm, love, and delight of heaven!

Heaven will be a place of reward. In His Sermon on the Mount, Jesus promised those who stay faithful while suffering for His sake that "a great reward awaits you in heaven" (Matthew 5:11,12). He taught His disciples to "store your treasures in heaven, where they will never become moth-eaten or rusty and where they will be safe from thieves" (Matthew 6:20).

Jesus also spoke in Luke 12:33 about the connection between faithful service on earth and rewards in heaven: "Sell what you have and give to those in need. This will store up treasure for you in heaven! And the purses of heaven have no holes in them. Your treasure will be safe." Believers will receive rewards for their righteous deeds (Matthew 10:42); for running the entire race without giving up (1 Corinthians 9:24,25); for cherishing and expecting Jesus' Second Coming (2 Timothy 4:7,8); for being faithful in testing (Revelation 2:10); and for all Spirit-led works glorifying God (Revelation 22:12).

Enthralled by the presence of the living Lord

and Savior, we will feel unworthy of any recognition. Knowing that He alone is worthy of all honor and attention, we will place at His feet any crowns of glory we may have earned (Revelation 4:10).

Heaven will be a place of unending worship. Heaven is where followers of the Savior of the world will have the privilege of giving to the Lord God all the worship that He alone deserves. It will be the most glorious worship service in all of eternity. No one will give any thought to an "order of service." No one will be conscious of any worship "style." The Father will set matters in order. The throne of God will be the focus of all eyes. The Spirit will prompt unending songs of praise from the lips of sinners saved by amazing grace. Believers from throughout the ages will come with Hosannas to the King of kings and Lord of lords, who is seated at the right hand of the Father.

The entire angelic host of heaven will proclaim, "You are worthy, O Lord, to receive glory and honor and power!" How great God is! Gathered by the stream flowing by the throne of God, the saved of all the earth will come face to face with their Redeemer. Each heart lifts in joy just to see Him, and to know that nothing will ever separate them again!

Furthermore, the angels of heaven will declare with a loud voice, "Worthy is the Lamb, who was slain, to receive power and wealth and wisdom and strength and honor and glory and praise!" (Revelation 5:12, NIV). Indeed, *all* living creatures will be drawn into praise of the Lord God. "I heard every creature in heaven and on earth and under the earth and on the sea, and all that is in them, singing, 'To Him who sits on the throne and to the Lamb be praise and honor and glory and power, for ever and ever'" (Revelation 5:13, NIV).

Revelation 15:2–4 describes God's redeemed singing in full chorus "the song of the Lamb":

> Great and marvelous are Your actions, Lord God Almighty. Just and true are Your ways, O King of the nations. Who will not fear, O Lord, and glorify Your name? For You alone are holy. All nations will come and worship before You, for Your righteous deeds have been revealed.

God the Father and Jesus will remain the focus of all praise. Rejoicing will seem unending.

Heaven will be a place where our knowledge of God will be complete. Can you imagine having all your spiritual questions answered satisfactorily? In heaven, we will see God face to face and will know Him as we are known (1 Corinthians 13:9–12). While the Bible has fully satisfied my questions regarding God's working in my life, perhaps you have unanswered questions you want to ask God as you stand before Him. Maybe you long for answers to all the questions you have had regarding why He permitted certain bad things to happen to you as part of His master plan. Rest assured that all of life's mysteries will be answered, and you will know God in the fullest possible way. How wonderful it will be to hear the wisdom of our great omniscient God! Heaven will be the greatest learning center of all eternity!

Heaven will be a place of newness, purity, and freedom. Revelation chapters 21 and 22 suggest that in heaven, we will feel as fresh as a newborn babe. We will be renewed, head to toe, heart and mind, soul and body, spirit and strength. There will be purity all around: pure air, pure water, pure hearts, crystal-clear minds. Righteousness will rule. Everything will be just right. No sin. No evil. No mistakes. No hurtful actions. No lack of faith in God. And, there will not be even a hint of that old sinful nature, the selfish flesh. The conflict in our hearts between flesh and Spirit will be over. We will be free, totally free, irrevocably set aside in white robes and cleansed consciences, utterly released from all

> *The conflict in our hearts between flesh and Spirit will be over.*

that beset us during our short time on earth.

There is no way to adequately describe all the ways our minds and bodies will enjoy heaven. But we can anticipate joyful feelings of delight. Think of the childhood glee of a roller-coaster or being tossed in the air by an uncle, or the sweet savors of holiday cooking, the soft perfumes of loved ones, the satisfaction of embraces. Imagine the security of all debts paid, of all duties done, of all anxieties vanished. Sexual activity will not be contemplated because our senses will be sated as never before by the mere presence of the Holy One. Jesus said, "In the resurrection there is no marriage; everyone is as the angels in heaven" (Matthew 22:30, TLB). God's love will be everywhere: in, around, and through us, one to another and to the Father and the Son and the Spirit who makes us one. Thank you, Lord Jesus!

Heaven will be a place of rest. As a place of rest, heaven will provide the believer complete escape from the punishment of hell. Hunger, thirst, sickness, pain, sorrow, tears, and trouble will be things of the past (Revelation 7:16,17; 21:4; 22:2). In heaven we will not feel a need to prevail over our troubles, for the Lamb will have won the victory over every challenge that once faced us on earth.

Never again shall we face a test or temptation.

Heaven

Never again shall the thought enter our minds of performing for anyone's acceptance. We shall fully know what it means to be accepted by God. Gone will be all sense of self-interest, self-promotion, or selfishness. We will be His and He will be ours. Resting in God, all will be complete. No more struggle. No more sorrow. No more ill treatment. No more abuse. No loss. No unexpected mishap.

There will be no need for us to plan, for everything is under God's control. We will be free to enjoy never-ending, unbroken joyous fellowship with our God and other believers.

On every level, heaven will be a place of rest from all the wearisome burdens we once carried on earth (Hebrews 4:9; Revelation 14:13). The promise of rest from all our earthly labors is perhaps one reason why the apostle Paul said that it was better to die and go on to be with the Lord, though he was willing to remain on earth for the benefit of the Church (Philippians 1:21–24).

Heaven is a place of continuing service to our great God. While heaven is a place of rest, it would be wrong for us to assume that we will be free to laze around all day. Be assured that God will have something meaningful for everyone to do.

For example, in Matthew 19:28, Jesus promises that His followers will join Him in governing heaven: "I assure you that when I, the Son of Man, sit upon My glorious throne in the Kingdom, you who have been My followers will also sit on twelve thrones, judging the twelve tribes of Israel."

The Book of Revelation clearly states that God's people shall participate in the royal work of heaven's temple: "They are standing in front of the throne of God, serving Him day and night in His temple" (7:15).

A similar passage, which likely refers to the same work of the temple, says: "No longer will there be any curse. The throne of God and of the Lamb will be in the city, and His servants will serve Him" (22:3, NIV).

Although heaven will be a place of eternal rest, it will not be a retirement center.

I conclude from these passages that heaven, although it will be a place of eternal rest, will not be a retirement center. We shall all take part in the rewarding work of serving our great God and Savior through the eternal ages. A detailed description of the exact job each of us shall perform in heaven is not made known in Scripture. But just the thought of serving our wondrous Master in any capacity thrills my heart beyond words.

Heaven is the place where we will meet Jesus of Nazareth face to face. What an astonishing opportunity!

Perhaps you have been in the presence of someone whose countenance and manner simply made you think of Jesus. I have. And, on a few occasions in my life, I have had the awesome, indescribable experience of sensing the very presence of God. One occurrence certainly was the night He gave me the vision of helping to fulfill the Great Commission throughout the world in what has become Campus Crusade for Christ.

Nevertheless, all my earthly experiences with God will not compare with the experience of entering heaven and coming into the presence of our Savior, the Lord Jesus Christ. In heaven there is no need for the sun; the Lamb Himself, the Light of the world, will illumine heaven and fill it with His warmth.

The apostle John's encounter in Revelation 1:13–18 begins to approach what may be our experience:

> And standing among them was one who looked like Jesus, who called Himself the Son of Man, wearing a long robe circled with a golden band across His chest. His hair was white as wool or snow, and His eyes penetrated like flames of fire. His feet gleamed like burnished bronze, and His voice thundered like the waves against the shore... His face

shone like the power of the sun in unclouded brilliance.

When I saw Him, I fell at His feet as dead; but He laid His right hand on me and said, "Don't be afraid! Though I am the First and the Last, the Living One who died, who is now alive forevermore, who has the keys of hell and death—don't be afraid!"

In heaven there will not be even a momentary loss of fellowship with the divine Captain of our Salvation, the ever-loving Father who seems everywhere hugging us, blessing us, and inviting us to enjoy Him forever. Ecstasy is a mere word on earth—seven letters, three syllables in English. But in heaven it will be the spine-tingling sensation of ultimate satisfaction created by the presence of our awesome God, the great I AM. We will be speechless. Words will not form to tell of Him. We can barely conceive of the brilliance of the Savior's appearing. Hallelujah to the Lamb!

Every tongue will confess, "Jesus Christ is Lord," to the glory of God the Father (Philippians 2:10, 11). We will proclaim in a glowing, flowing shout of praise from our hearts that Jesus Christ is Lord: We exalt you, Lord. You are awesome. We love you. We thank you. Hallelujah! For the Lord God Omnipotent reigns forever and ever! Amen!

Heaven

THE GREAT CITY

The splendor of heaven astounds the mind. While the preceding description of heaven should make us long to be there, I would be remiss if I did not mention one of heaven's most prominent features —the holy city, the new Jerusalem. The city, described in Revelation chapter 21, comes down "out of heaven" and is approximately 1,400 miles long by 1,400 miles wide by 1,400 miles high. If these distances were interpreted literally, this city would be approximately 739,200 stories tall and cover an area of nearly two million square miles. It would allow comfortable, resplendent quarters for everyone who has ever lived!

Scripture describes the holy city as "filled with the glory of God." It is a breathtaking place that will sparkle "like a precious gem, crystal clear like jasper," and it will be "like a beautiful bride prepared for her husband." The foundation stones of the city wall will be adorned with all kinds of precious stones. Each of the twelve gates of the city will be made of one pearl. The walls of the city will be 200 feet thick, made of jasper. The street will be of a unique gold, pure and virtually transparent. Beside the tree of life, flowing from the "throne of God and of the Lamb," will be the crystal clear river of the water of life (Revelation 22:1).

Our God goes first class! No expense will be spared.

What Leads to Heaven

With its glory and splendor, heaven is a marvelous place. We should look forward to it with eager anticipation. There is only *one* way to have eternal life in heaven: we each must receive Jesus Christ. He is Savior and Lord. The Bible says, "And this is what God has testified: He has given us eternal life, and this life is in his Son. So whoever has God's Son has life; whoever does not have his Son does not have life" (1 John 5:11,12).

There is only one way to have eternal life in heaven: receive Jesus Christ as Savior and Lord.

I urge you, dear reader, to ask yourself this question: "Have I turned from my sins and asked Jesus of Nazareth to forgive me of them and to help me follow Him in spirit and in truth?" If not, permit me to share three important things Jesus did to provide you with eternal life.

First, He lived the perfect life that the Ten Commandments requires of every person. Everyone is responsible to live a spotless life before God's holy standards. Yet the Bible says that "all have sinned; all fall short of God's glorious standard" (Romans 3:23). This is why Jesus lived the Law's requirements for us, thus fulfilling its righteous demands (Matthew 5:17).

Second, Jesus died for our sins. The Bible tells us, "Without the shedding of blood, there is no forgiveness of sins" (Hebrews 9:22). By His death, Christ shed His blood to pay the penalty for our rebellion against God's Holy Law (Romans 5:8; Hebrews 9:15). Now we do not have to pay the penalty for our sins, but instead can enjoy eternity with Him. He died to provide forgiveness for the rich and poor, the old and young, the religious and irreligious.

Third, He rose victoriously from the tomb, having conquered sin and death. Because Jesus rose from the dead, death can no longer hold anyone in its grip who trusts in His name (1 Corinthians 15:1–8; Romans 6:4–10). We can know eternal life without cost.

How does Christ's perfect work become practical for us? We do not receive salvation by joining a church, having godly parents, or even knowing *about* Jesus. The Bible tells us we must "receive" Him (John 1:12, NIV). In other words, God calls us to place our trust in Jesus, believing that what He did in His life, death, and resurrection, He did for us personally (Romans 3:22,25). Turning from our sins and trusting in Christ's work on our behalf is *all* we will ever need to receive the gift of eternal life.

When we receive Christ, God provides us with His Spirit so we can overcome sin in our lives and thus walk with a consistent step in His marvelous kingdom of light. Because we are now *of* the light, we are to walk *in* the light (1 John 1:7).

Your Choice

We have looked at the glories of heaven. We have looked at the gloominess of hell. Now, if you have not already done so, it is time for you to choose which one of these places you want to go to when you die. Would you like to take this opportunity to settle the question of where you will spend eternity, once and for all? Perhaps you remain unconvinced of the realities of hell. But even if there is a *remote* possibility that there is a burning hell, do you dare take this chance? What do you possibly have to lose by receiving Christ and knowing for sure that He has eliminated even the faintest possibility that you could go to hell? My urgent prayer is that you will choose Jesus and heaven, and that you will help countless others make the same decision so that they too may "live in the house of the LORD forever" (Psalm 23:6).

Prayer is talking with God. Why not talk with Him right now and express your desire to become His child? God knows your heart and is not as concerned with your words as He is with the attitude of your heart. The following is a suggested prayer:

Heaven

Lord Jesus, I need You. I acknowledge that I have sinned against You. Thank You for dying on the cross for my sins and rising from the dead to give me eternal life. I open the door of my heart and receive You as my Savior and Lord. Take control of the throne of my life. Make me the kind of person You want me to be.

If you prayed that prayer with a believing heart, God heard and answered your prayer. This day you have begun the most exciting, fulfilling adventure one can ever experience. You have become a part of His eternal family, and heaven is your home! But this is just the beginning. In order to experience a bit of heaven here on earth, there are basic truths you need to know. Read Appendix B to learn how to be filled and directed by God's Holy Spirit. Also, please write to me at bbright@ccci.org so that I can send you important materials that will assist you in your great, exciting journey with our Lord Jesus Christ.

APPENDIX A

Would You Like to Know God Personally?

The following four principles will help you discover how to know God personally and experience the abundant life He promised.

1 *God **loves** you and created you to know Him personally.*

God's Love
"God so loved the world that He gave His only begotten Son, that whoever believes in Him should not perish, but have eternal life" (John 3:16).

God's Plan
"Now this is eternal life: that they may know you, the only true God, and Jesus Christ, whom you have sent" (John 17:3).

What prevents us from knowing God personally?

2 *Man is **sinful** and **separated** from God, so we cannot know Him personally or experience His love.*

Man Is Sinful

"All have sinned and fall short of the glory of God" (Romans 3:23).

Man was created to have fellowship with God; but, because of his own stubborn self-will, he chose to go his own independent way and fellowship with God was broken. This self-will, characterized by an attitude of active rebellion or passive indifference, is an evidence of what the Bible calls sin.

Man Is Separated

"The wages of sin is death" [spiritual separation from God] (Romans 6:23).

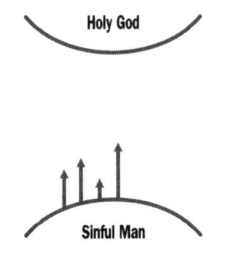

This diagram illustrates that God is holy and man is sinful. A great gulf separates the two. The arrows illustrate that man is continually trying to reach God and establish a personal relationship with Him through his own efforts, such as a good life, philosophy, or religion —but he inevitably fails.

The third principle explains the only way to bridge this gulf...

Would You Like to Know God Personally?

3 *Jesus Christ is God's **only** provision for man's sin. Through Him alone we can know God personally and experience God's love.*

He Died In Our Place

"God demonstrates His own love toward us, in that while we were yet sinners, Christ died for us" (Romans 5:8).

He Rose From the Dead

"Christ died for our sins...He was buried...He was raised on the third day according to the Scriptures ...He appeared to Peter, then to the twelve. After that He appeared to more than five hundred..." (1 Corinthians 15:3–6).

He Is the Only Way to God

"Jesus said to him, 'I am the way, and the truth, and the life; no one comes to the Father, but through Me'" (John 14:6).

This diagram illustrates that God has bridged the gulf that separates us from Him by sending His Son, Jesus Christ, to die on the cross in our place to pay the penalty for our sins.

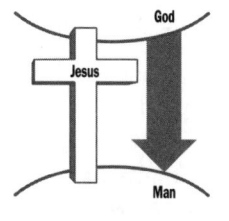

It is not enough just to know these three truths...

Heaven or Hell

4 *We must individually **receive** Jesus Christ as Savior and Lord; then we can know God personally and experience His love.*

We Must Receive Christ
"As many as received Him, to them He gave the right to become children of God, even to those who believe in His name" (John 1:12).

We Receive Christ Through Faith
"By grace you have been saved through faith; and that not of yourselves, it is the gift of God; not as a result of works that no one should boast" (Ephesians 2:8,9).

When We Receive Christ, We Experience a New Birth (Read John 3:1–8.)

We Receive Christ By Personal Invitation
[Christ speaking] "Behold, I stand at the door and knock; if anyone hears My voice and opens the door, I will come in to him" (Revelation 3:20).

Receiving Christ involves turning to God from self (repentance) and trusting Christ to come into our lives to forgive us of our sins and to make us what He wants us to be. Just to agree intellectually that Jesus Christ is the Son of God and that He died on the cross for our sins is not enough. Nor is it enough

Would You Like to Know God Personally?

to have an emotional experience. We receive Jesus Christ by faith, as an act of our will.

These two circles represent two kinds of lives:

Self-Directed Life
- **S** – Self is on the throne
- **†** – Christ is outside the life
- ● – Interests are directed by self, often resulting in discord and frustration

Christ-Directed Life
- **†** – Christ is in the life and on the throne
- **S** – Self is yielding to Christ
- ● – Interests are directed by Christ, resulting in harmony with God's plan

Which circle best represents your life?
Which circle would you like to have represent your life?

The following explains how you can receive Christ:

You Can Receive Christ Right Now by Faith Through Prayer *(Prayer is talking with God)*

God knows your heart and is not so concerned with your words as He is with the attitude of your heart. The following is a suggested prayer:

Lord Jesus, I need You. Thank You for dying on the cross for my sins. I open the door of my life and receive You as my Savior and Lord. Thank You for forgiving my sins and giving me eternal life. Take control of the throne of my life. Make me the kind of person You want me to be.

Does this prayer express the desire of your heart?

If it does, I invite you to pray this prayer right now, and Christ will come into your life, as He promised.

How to Know That Christ Is in Your Life
Did you receive Christ into your life? According to His promise in Revelation 3:20, where is Christ right now in relation to you? Christ said that He would come into your life and be your friend so you can know Him personally. Would He mislead you? On what authority do you know that God has answered your prayer? (The trustworthiness of God Himself and His Word.)

The Bible Promises Eternal Life to All Who Receive Christ
"God has given us eternal life, and this life is in His Son. He who has the Son has the life; he who does not have the Son of God does not have the life. These things I have written to you who believe in the name of the Son of God, in order that you may know that you have eternal life" (1 John 5:11–13).

Thank God often that Christ is in your life and that He will never leave you (Hebrews 13:5). You can know on the basis of His promise that Christ lives in you and that you have eternal life from the very moment you invite Him in. He will not deceive you.

An important reminder…

Would You Like to Know God Personally?

Do Not Depend on Feelings

The promise of God's Word, the Bible—not our feelings—is our authority. The Christian lives by faith (trust) in the trustworthiness of God Himself and His Word. This diagram illustrates the relationship among *fact* (God and His Word), *faith* (our trust in God and His Word), and *feeling* (the result of our faith and obedience). (Read John 14:21.)

The train will run with or without the caboose. However, it would be useless to attempt to pull the train by the caboose. In the same way, as Christians we do not depend on feelings or emotions, but we place our faith (trust) in the trustworthiness of God and the promises of His Word.

Now That You Have Entered Into a Personal Relationship With Christ

The moment you received Christ by faith, as an act of the will, many things happened, including:

- Christ came into your life (Revelation 3:20 and Colossians 1:27).
- Your sins were forgiven (Colossians 1:14).
- You became a child of God (John 1:12).
- You received eternal life (John 5:24).

- You began the great adventure for which God created you (John 10:10; 2 Corinthians 5:17; 1 Thessalonians 5:18).

Can you think of anything more wonderful that could happen to you than entering into a personal relationship with Christ? Would you like to thank God in prayer right now for what He has done for you? By thanking God, you demonstrate your faith.

To enjoy your new relationship with God…

Suggestions for Christian Growth

Spiritual growth results from trusting Jesus Christ. "The righteous man shall live by faith" (Galatians 3:11). A life of faith will enable you to practice the following:

- G *Go* to God in prayer daily (John 15:7).
- R *Read* God's Word daily (Acts 17:11); begin with the Gospel of John.
- O *Obey* God moment by moment (John 14:21).
- W *Witness* for Christ by your life and words (Matthew 4:19; John 15:8).
- T *Trust* God for every detail of your life (1 Peter 5:7).
- H *Holy Spirit*—allow Him to control and empower your daily life and witness (Galatians 5:16,17; Acts 1:8).

Fellowship in a Good Church

God's Word admonishes us not to forsake "the assembling of ourselves together..." (Hebrews 10:25). Several logs burn brightly together, but put one aside on the cold hearth and the fire goes out. So it is with your relationship with other Christians. If you do not belong to a church, do not wait to be invited. Take the initiative; call the pastor of a nearby church where Christ is honored and His Word is preached. Start this week, and make plans to attend regularly.

APPENDIX B

The Spirit-filled Life

Every day can be an exciting adventure for the Christian who knows the reality of being filled with the Holy Spirit and who lives constantly, moment by moment, under His gracious direction.

The Bible tells us that there are three kinds of people:

1. **Natural Man:** One who has not received Christ.

   Self-Directed Life
   S – Self is on the throne
   † – Christ is outside the life
   ● – Interests are directed by self, often resulting in discord and frustration

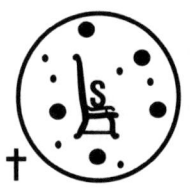

   "A natural man does not accept the things of the Spirit of God; for they are foolishness to him, and he cannot understand them, because they are spiritually appraised" (1 Corinthians 2:14, NASB).

HEAVEN OR HELL

2. **Spiritual Man:** One who is directed and empowered by the Holy Spirit.

    Christ-Directed Life
    † – Christ is in the life and on the throne
    S – Self is yielding to Christ
    • – Interests are directed by Christ, resulting in harmony with God's plan

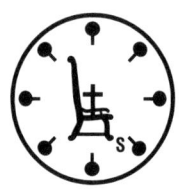

    "He who is spiritual appraises all things" (1 Corinthians 2:15, NASB).

3. **Carnal Man:** One who has received Christ, but who lives in defeat because he trusts in his own efforts to live the Christian life.

    Self-Directed Life
    S – Self is on the throne
    † – Christ dethroned and not allowed to direct the life
    • – Interests are directed by self, often resulting in discord and frustration

    "I, brethren, could not speak to you as to spiritual people but as to carnal, as to babes in Christ. I fed you with milk and not with solid food; for until now you were not able to receive it, and even now you are still not

The Spirit-filled Life

able; for you are still carnal. For when there are envy, strife, and divisions among you, are you not carnal and behaving like mere men?" (1 Corinthians 3:1–3).

The following are four principles for living the Spirit-filled life:

1. God has provided for us an abundant and fruitful Christian life.

"Jesus said, 'I have come that they may have life, and that they may have it more abundantly'" (John 10:10, NKJ).

"The fruit of the Spirit is love, joy, peace, patience, kindness, goodness, faithfulness, gentleness, self-control; against such things is no law" (Galatians 5:22,23).

Read John 15:5 and Acts 1:8.

The following are some personal traits of the spiritual man that result from trusting God:

- Love
- Joy
- Peace
- Patience
- Kindness
- Faithfulness
- Goodness

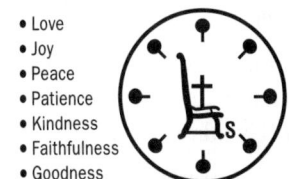

- Life is Christ-centered
- Empowered by Holy Spirit
- Introduces others to Christ
- Has effective prayer life
- Understands God's Word
- Trusts God
- Obeys God

The degree to which these traits are manifested in the life depends on the extent to which the Christian trusts the Lord with every detail of his life, and on his maturity in Christ. One who is only beginning to understand the ministry of the Holy Spirit should not be discouraged if he is not as fruitful as more mature Christians who have known and experienced this truth for a longer period.

Why is it that most Christians are not experiencing the abundant life?

2 Carnal Christians cannot experience the abundant and fruitful Christian life.

The carnal man trusts in his own efforts to live the Christian life:

- He is either uninformed about, or has forgotten, God's love, forgiveness, and power (Romans 5:8–10; Hebrews 10:1–25; 1 John 1; 2:1–3; 2 Peter 1:9).

- He has an up-and-down spiritual experience.

- He wants to do what is right, but cannot.

- He fails to draw on the power of the Holy Spirit to live the Christian life (1 Corinthians 3:1–3; Romans 7:15–24; 8:7; Galatians 5:16–18).

Some or all of the following traits may characterize

The Spirit-filled Life

the carnal man—the Christian who does not fully trust God:

- Legalistic attitude
- Impure thoughts
- Jealousy
- Guilt
- Worry
- Discouragement
- Critical spirit
- Frustration

- Aimlessness
- Fear
- Ignorance of his spiritual heritage
- Unbelief
- Disobedience
- Loss of love for God and for others
- Poor prayer life
- No desire for Bible study

(The individual who professes to be a Christian but who continues to practice sin should realize that he may not be a Christian at all, according to 1 John 2:3; 3:6–9; and Ephesians 5:5.)

The third truth gives us the only solution to this problem...

3 Jesus promised the abundant and fruitful life as the result of being filled (directed and empowered) by the Holy Spirit.

The Spirit-filled life is the Christ-directed life by which Christ lives His life in and through us in the power of the Holy Spirit (John 15).

- One becomes a Christian through the ministry of the Holy Spirit (John 3:1–8.) From the moment of spiritual birth, the Christian is indwelt by the Holy Spirit at all times (John 1:12; Colossians 2:9,10; John 14:16,17).

All Christians are indwelt by the Holy Spirit, but not all Christians are filled (directed, controlled, and empowered) by the Holy Spirit on an ongoing basis.

- The Holy Spirit is the source of the overflowing life (John 7:37–39).
- In His last command before His ascension, Christ promised the power of the Holy Spirit to enable us to be witnesses for Him (Acts 1:1–9).

How, then, can one be filled with the Holy Spirit?

4 We are filled (directed and empowered) by the Holy Spirit by faith; then we can experience the abundant and fruitful life that Christ promised to each Christian.

You can appropriate the filling of the Holy Spirit right now if you:

- Sincerely desire to be directed and empowered by the Holy Spirit (Matthew 5:6; John 7:37–39).
- Confess your sins. By faith, thank God that He has forgiven all of your sins—past, present, and future—because Christ died for you (Colossians 2:13–15).

The Spirit-filled Life

- Present every area of your life to God (Romans 12:1,2).
- By faith claim the fullness of the Holy Spirit, according to:

  His command: Be filled with the Spirit. "Do not get drunk on wine, which leads to debauchery. Instead, be filled with the Spirit" (Ephesians 5:18).

  His promise: He will always answer when we pray according to His will. "This is the confidence we have in approaching God: that if we ask anything according to his will, he hears us. And if we know that He hears us—whatever we ask—we know that we have what we asked of Him" (1 John 5:14,15).

How to Pray in Faith to be Filled With the Holy Spirit

We are filled with the Holy Spirit by faith alone. However, true prayer is one way of expressing your faith. The following is a suggested prayer:

> Dear Father, I need You. I acknowledge that I have been directing my own life and that, as a result, I have sinned against You. I thank You that You have forgiven my sins through

Christ's death on the cross for me. I now invite Christ to again take His place on the throne of my life. Fill me with the Holy Spirit as You *commanded* me to be filled, and as You *promised* in Your Word that You would do if I asked in faith. I pray this in the name of Jesus. As an expression of my faith, I now thank You for directing my life and for filling me with the Holy Spirit.

Does this prayer express the desire of your heart? If so, bow in prayer and trust God to fill you with the Holy Spirit right now.

End Notes

1. The capitalization of "Satan" traditionally has been required as a matter of grammar; proper names must be capitalized. But it grates against everything within me that his name ever be capitalized. He is a convicted murderer, liar, thief, accuser of the family of God, and stirrer of strife (Revelation 12:10). There should never be any possible way—even in grammar—in which he is treated in the same way as our great Creator God and Savior, the Lord Jesus Christ. Nonetheless, I defer to the pattern of professional grammar so that this book not be seen as ungrammatical.

2. Martyn Lloyd-Jones, *Spiritual Depression* (Grand Rapids, MI: William B. Eerdmans Publishing Co., 1965), 35.

3. Cited by Leland Ryken, James C. Wilhoit, Tremper Longman III, gen. eds., *Dictionary of Biblical Imagery* (Downers Grove, IL: InterVarsity Press, 1998), 377.

4. Wayne Grudem, *Bible Doctrines: Essential Teachings of the Christian Faith* (Grand Rapids, MI: Zondervan Publishing House, 1999), 176, 459.

5. Jonathan Edwards, quoted by Edward William Fudge,

The Fire That Consumes (Houston: Providential Press, 1982), 417.

6. *Dictionary of Biblical Imagery*, 377.
7. Elliot Miller, "Evangelicals and the Annihilationism of Hell" (*Christian Research Journal*, Summer 1991), 8.
8. *Dictionary of Biblical Imagery*, 377.
9. Ibid.
10. Ibid.
11. Ibid.
12. Cathy Lynn Grossman, "A Measure of Faith" religious survey (*USA Today*, Dec. 24, 2001), D-4.
13. Charles Spurgeon, *C. H. Spurgeon's Prayers*, cited in *Facing Forever* (Wake Forest, NC: Church Initiative, 2001), 29.
14. Don Wyrtzen and L. E. Singer, "Finally Home" (Singspiration Music, 1971).
15. J. I. Packer, *Keep in Step with the Spirit* (Tappan, NJ: Fleming H. Revell Co., Baker Book House, 1987).

Resources by Bill Bright

BOOKS

Beyond All Limits *(co-author)*
Blessed Child *(co-author)*
Building a Home in a Pull-Apart World
Child of the King, A *(co-author)*
Come Help Change the World
The Coming Revival *(1996 Gold Medallion Finalist)*
First Love
GOD: Discover His Character
The Greatest Lesson I've Ever Learned *(Series Editor)*
Handbook of Concepts for Living
Holy Spirit: Key to Supernatural Living
Life Without Equal
Living Supernaturally in Christ
Man Without Equal
Promises: A Daily Guide for Supernatural Living
Quiet Moments with Bill Bright
Red Sky in the Morning *(co-author)*
The Secret

The Transforming Power of Fasting & Prayer
Witnessing Without Fear *(1988 Gold Medallion Award Winner)*
Written by the Hand of God

TRANSFERABLE CONCEPTS

How You Can Be Sure You Are a Christian
How You Can Experience Gods Love & Forgiveness
How You Can Be Filled With the Spirit
How You Can Walk in the Spirit
How You Can Be a Fruitful Witness
How You Can Introduce Others to Christ
How You Can Help Fulfill the Great Commission
How You Can Love By Faith
How You Can Pray With Confidence
How You Can Experience the Adventure of Giving
How You Can Study the Bible Effectively

TEN BASIC STEPS

Introduction: Uniqueness of Jesus
Step 1: The Christian Adventure
Step 2: The Christian and Abundant Life
Step 3: The Christian and the Holy Spirit
Step 4: The Christian and Prayer
Step 5: The Christian and the Bible
Step 6: The Christian and Obedience
Step 7: The Christian and Witnessing

Resources

Step 8: The Christian and Giving
Step 9: Exploring the Old Testament
Step 10: Exploring the New Testament
Ten Basic Steps Leader's Guide
Handbook for Christian Maturity

OTHER STUDY MATERIALS

Change Your World Through Fasting & Prayer *(Leader's Guide & Study Guide)*
Five Steps of Christian Growth *(Leader's Guide & Study Guide)*
Five Steps to Fasting & Prayer *(Leader's Guide & Study Guide)*
Five Steps to Knowing God's Will *(Leader's Guide & Study Guide)*
Five Steps to Making Disciples *(Leader's Guide & Study Guide)*
Five Steps to Sharing Your Faith *(Leader's Guide & Study Guide)*
GOD: Discover His Character *(Leader's Guide & Study Guide)*
How to Reach Your World for Christ Through a New Life Group *(Leader's Guide & Study Guide)*
Preparing for the Coming Revival *(Leader's Guide & Study Guide)*
Reaching Your World Through Witnessing Without Fear *(Facilitator's Guide & Participant's Manual)*

Tracts & Booklets

Beginning Your Journey of Joy *(co-author)*
Bilingual Four Spiritual Laws *(Spanish/English)*
Connecting with God *(student version of 4 Laws)*
The Four Spiritual Laws
GOD: Discover the Benefits of His Attributes Card
GOD: 13 Steps to Discovering His Attributes
GOD: Knowing Him by His Names
GOD: Seeking Him Wholeheartedly
A Great Adventure
Have You Made the Wonderful Discovery of the Spirit-filled Life?
Jesus & the Intellectual
Keys to Dynamic Living Card
Living Supernaturally in Christ: The Supernatural You
Living Supernaturally in Christ: Why Do Christians Suffer?
Satisfied? *(4-color version of Spirit-filled Life)*
7 Steps to Successful Fasting & Prayer
Would You Like to Belong to God's Family?
Would You Like to Know God Personally?
Your 5 Duties as a Christian Citizen
Your Most Important Investment

William R. Bright
*Founder, Chairman, and President Emeritus,
Campus Crusade for Christ International*

From a small beginning in 1951, the organization he began now has a presence in 196 countries in areas representing 99.6% of the world's population. Campus Crusade for Christ has more than 70 ministries and major projects, utilizing more than 25,000 full-time and 500,000 trained volunteer staff. Each ministry is designed to help fulfill the Great Commission, Christ's command to help carry the gospel of God's love and forgiveness in Christ to every person on earth.

Born in Coweta, Oklahoma, on October 19, 1921, Bright graduated with honors from Northeastern State University, and completed five years of graduate study at Princeton and Fuller Theological Seminaries. He holds five honorary doctorates from prestigious institutions and has received numerous other recognitions, including the ECPA Gold Medallion Lifetime Achievement Award (2001), the Golden Angel Award as International Churchman of the Year (1982), and the $1.1 million Templeton Prize for Progress in Religion (1996), which he dedicated to promoting fasting and prayer throughout the world. He has received the first-ever Lifetime Achievement Award from his alma mater (2001).

Bright has authored more than 100 books, booklets, videos and audio tapes, as well as thousands of articles and pamphlets, some of which have been printed in most major languages and distributed by the millions. Among his books are: *Come Help Change the World, The Secret, The Holy Spirit, A Man Without Equal, A Life Without Equal, The Coming Revival, The Transforming Power of Fasting & Prayer, Red Sky in the Morning* (co-author), *GOD: Discover His Character, Living Supernaturally in Christ*, and the booklet *Have You Heard of the Four Spiritual Laws?* (which has an estimated 2.5 billion circulation).

He has also been responsible for many individual initiatives in ministry, particularly in evangelism. For example, the *JESUS* film, which he conceived and financed through Campus Crusade, has, by latest estimates, been viewed by over 4.6 billion people in 236 nations and provinces.

Bright and his wife, Vonette, who assisted him in founding Campus Crusade for Christ, live in Orlando, Florida. Their two sons, Zac and Brad, and their wives, Terry and Katherine, are also in full-time Christian ministry.